Anglican Foundations Series

Dearly Beloved

Building God's People Through Morning and Evening Prayer

By Mark Burkill

The Latimer Trust

Dearly Beloved: Building God's People Through Morning and Evening Prayer © Mark Burkill 2012

ISBN 978-1-906327-10-1

Cover photo © Ingo Bartussek - Fotolia.com

Quotations from the Bible are taken from the Holy Bible, New International Version® Anglicized, NIV® Copyright © 1979, 1984, 2011 by Biblica, Inc.® Used by permission. All rights reserved worldwide.

Published by the Latimer Trust August 2012

The Latimer Trust (formerly Latimer House, Oxford) is a conservative Evangelical research organisation within the Church of England, whose main aim is to promote the history and theology of Anglicanism as understood by those in the Reformed tradition. Interested readers are welcome to consult its website for further details of its many activities.

The Latimer Trust
c/o Oak Hill College
London N14 4PS UK
Registered Charity: 1084337
Company Number: 4104465
Web: www.latimertrust.org
E-mail: administrator@latimertrust.org

Views expressed in works published by The Latimer Trust are those of the authors and do not necessarily represent the official position of The Latimer Trust

Foreword to the Anglican Foundations Series

The celebration of the 350th anniversary of the 1662 *Book of Common Prayer* has helped to stimulate a renewed interest in its teaching and fundamental contribution to Anglican identity. Archbishop Cranmer and others involved in the English Reformation knew well that the content and shape of the services set out in the Prayer Book were vital ways of teaching congregations biblical truth and the principles of the Christian gospel. This basic idea of *'lex orandi, lex credendi'* is extremely important. For good or ill, the content and shape of our meetings as Christians is highly influential in shaping our practice in following the Lord Jesus Christ.

Furthermore, increased interest in the historic formularies of the Church of England has been generated by the current painful divisions within the Anglican Communion which inevitably highlight the matter of Anglican identity. In the end our Anglican Foundations cannot be avoided since our identity as Anglicans is intimately related to the question of Christian identity, and Christian identity cannot avoid questions of Christian understanding and belief. While the 39 Articles often become the focus of discussions about Christian and Anglican belief (and have been addressed in this series through *The Faith We Confess* by Gerald Bray) the fact that the 1662 *Book of Common Prayer* and *The Ordinal* are also part of the doctrinal foundations of the Church of England is often neglected.

Thus the aim of this series of booklets, which focus on the Formularies of the Church of England and the elements of the different services within the Prayer Book, is to highlight what those services teach about the Christian faith and to demonstrate how they are also designed to shape the practice of that faith. As well as providing an account of the origins of the Prayer Book services, these booklets are designed to offer practical guidance on how such services may be used in Christian ministry nowadays.

It is not necessary to use the exact 1662 services in order to be true to our Anglican heritage, identity and formularies. However if we grasp the principles of Cranmer which underpinned those services then modern versions of them can fulfil the same task of teaching congregations how to live as Christians which Cranmer intended. If we are ignorant of the principles of Cranmer then our

Sunday gatherings will inevitably teach something to Anglican congregations, but it will not be the robust biblical faith which Cranmer promoted.

So our hope is that through this Anglican Foundations series our identity as Anglicans will be clarified and that there will be by God's grace a renewal of the teaching and practice of the Christian faith through the services of the Church of England and elsewhere within the Anglican Communion.

Mark Burkill and Gerald Bray

Series Editors, The Latimer Trust

CONTENTS

1. Preface 1
2. Meetings in the early and medieval church and their relevance 10
3. Cranmer's Reform 16
4. After Cranmer 28
5. The Modern Era 36
6. What Now? 44

1. Preface

There has always been confusion about the proper purpose, significance and conduct of Christian meetings. Yet we may not realise that this is no light matter. In 1 Corinthians 11:17 the apostle Paul says 'In the following directives I have no praise for you, for your meetings do more harm than good'. This may surprise us. Paul is saying that when we gather as Christians, whether we call those occasions services, meetings or worship, it is possible that our meetings do more harm than good. We must at least entertain the possibility that it would be better if we did not meet together if we are not fulfilling the Lord's will and purpose for our meetings.

This booklet is focussing on the content and intent of those services entitled 'Morning Prayer' and 'Evening Prayer' in the 1662 *Book of Common Prayer*. If we say that we are Anglicans then we need to be aware of Cranmer's rationale for these services and why the elements within them are there. We need to be aware of these things because the *Book of Common Prayer* remains one of the key formularies of the Church of England. We need to be aware of these matters because if our meetings are not shaped by Cranmer's biblical rationale then they will certainly be shaped by something else.

Many surveys of Church of England practice since the Reformation point out that up until relatively recently the normal diet for Church of England congregations on Sundays was Morning and Evening Prayer[1]. These were also known as Mattins or Evensong. It was only in the middle of the last century under the influence of the

---

[1] James White, *Brief History of Christian Worship* (Nashville: Abingdon Press, 1993) p 119. Jeremy Gregory, 'The Prayer Book and the Parish Church: From the Restoration to the Oxford Movement' in C Hefling and C Shattuck (eds.), *The Oxford Guide to the Book of Common Prayer* (Oxford: OUP, 2006) p 96.

Parish Communion movement that this pattern changed[2]. Even today it is derivatives of Morning and Evening Prayer that form the basis of the normal evangelical Sunday meeting in the Church of England and elsewhere in the Anglican Communion. If we are to be true to our Anglican and Scriptural heritage it may not be necessary to use the 1662 *Book of Common Prayer* today but it is essential that its principles and rationale shape our practice.

Nonetheless the reality is that there is enormous confusion over the purpose of Christian meetings at the present time. There is a confusion over terminology and a confusion over theology. It is only by re-examining the biblical use of certain words and appreciating the biblical understanding of the Christian life that these confusions may be dispelled.

Howard Marshall laid the foundations for dispelling the confusion over terminology, but the ingrained misunderstanding is so prevalent that his points need to be stressed repeatedly[3]. Marshall points out that as used today, 'the terms 'worship' and 'service' strongly suggest that the central thing that takes place when Christians gather together is that they do something which is addressed in some way to God'[4]. While Marshall acknowledges that the whole of the Christian life must be one of worship and that this therefore includes those times when Christians gather together, he insists that the New Testament evidence demonstrates that it is not the case that 'the purpose of Christian meetings was understood as being primarily and directly worship, homage and adoration addressed to God'[5]. Of course this conclusion will apply to all meetings whether or not they include Holy Communion.

---

[2] Kenneth Stevenson, *Family Services* (London: SPCK, 1981 Alcuin Club no3) p1. *Prayer Book Revision in the Church of England* (London: SPCK, 1958) p23. Colin Buchanan, 'The Winds of Change' in *The Oxford Guide to the Book of Common Prayer* p233.

[3] I Howard Marshall, 'How far did the early Christians worship God?' *Churchman* 1985 vol 99 pp 216-229.

[4] Ibid., p 216.

[5] Ibid., p 226.

Thus Marshall insists that although there are other elements in church meetings, the primary element needs to be seen as being from God to man. Viewing meetings as being primarily about God speaking with and dealing with human beings is why he regards the use of terms like 'worship' and 'service' as being so misleading.

Normally those terms imply that we are meeting in order to offer something to God. He would therefore prefer that the terms 'church meeting' or 'assembly' be used. These words allow us to fill them with a meaning in which teaching and building (edification) are primary, with this proclamation of the Word leading to response to the Word[6]. We will see that Cranmer understood this biblical focus that Marshall describes very clearly.

There is of course a solid theological reason for this pattern of the use of words that Marshall expounds. Vaughan Roberts puts it well when he says that we misunderstand the purpose of our meetings so badly because 'we are still stuck in the Old Testament in our thinking. We have failed to grasp the significance of the coming of Jesus'[7]. Similarly David Peterson says that 'The gospel is key to the New Testament teaching about worship'[8]. He expands the significance of this by stating that fundamentally 'worship' in the New Testament means believing the gospel and responding with one's whole life and being to the work of Christ in the power of the Spirit. Then, significantly for our understanding of the purpose of our Christian meetings, Peterson further stresses that if Christians are to serve God in their everyday lives they need to be exposed to an on-going, gospel based ministry of teaching and exhortation. Thus the purpose of Christian gatherings is the edification or building of the body of Christ. Even when we pray and sing in the congregation,

---

[6] Ibid., p 228.
[7] Vaughan Roberts, *True Worship* (Carlisle: Paternoster, 2002) p 31.
[8] David Peterson, *Engaging with God* (Leicester: IVP, 1992) p 287.

edification is to be our concern.⁹ This emphasis on edification which stresses the way we gather to hear God speak to us as human beings of course should not be viewed as excluding the human response to God within our meetings. However unless the primary concern for edification is recognised then whatever theoretical nuances about the response element in our meetings we may make, the practical outcome will be confusion in those meetings about what we are there for.

In sum, we must recognise that the Bible alerts us to the fact that we must be very careful about using words like 'worship' and 'service' because they can be so misleading and so distant from the New Testament understanding of the purpose of our meetings (note the way these words are used in Romans 12:1-2 and Ephesians 4:11-13). While all of life is indeed our worship and service of God, and that includes the times when we gather together as Christians, the purpose of such gatherings is for God to edify his people and not primarily to make any offering to him.

Nevertheless we would be faithful to Cranmer himself in recognising that current confusion does not compel us to give up entirely on using words like 'worship' or 'service' to describe our meetings together. Cranmer was always ready to try and work at rejuvenating existing practices by filling them with biblical content. Even though we may be tempted to abandon a word like 'worship' in reference to our Christian meetings, Carson points out that we would then still have to find a new word to describe our activities when we

---

[9] Peterson pp 286-287. Note though that even this concern for edification may be misunderstood. Philip Jensen reminds us that the edification activity is ultimately directed towards the heavenly gathering or church, rather than specifically the local or earthly gathering. He also alerts us to the way that if edification is seen as simply 'building up' then it can make church meetings and activities very inward looking. It is building in all directions. See Philip Jensen, 'What is Church for?' *The Briefing (UK edition)* vol 397 (January/February 2012) pp 14-21.

meet together corporately.[10] It is sometimes more fruitful to work at reclaiming a word than to introduce a new one.

More substantially however, when we look at contemporary understandings of what we are doing when we meet together as Church of England congregations, we see that these gospel and Bible emphases which Cranmer himself grasped so clearly are largely ignored.

Morning and Evening Prayer as we have them in the 1662 Prayer Book were created by Cranmer through adapting earlier patterns of daily prayer which were also known as the Divine Office. In his book *Daily Liturgical Prayer: Origins and Theology* Gregory Woolfenden concludes his survey by stating that from the late Middle Ages there have been two fundamental theologies of daily prayer. One seeks to enact and express the Christian mystery of Redemption and so inspire the faithful to praise and prayer. The other, which he says is more characteristic of the Renaissance and Reformation periods, can be viewed as a theology of the divine office in which scripture is inculcated so as to support a powerful and formative spirituality.[11] Thus on the one hand there is a theology in which Christians meet to offer praise and prayer to God, and on the other a theology in which Christians meet in order to be shaped by God speaking the gospel to us.

Inculcating Scripture as the basis for a powerful spirituality would be a fair summary of what Cranmer aimed to achieve through Morning and Evening Prayer, yet it has always been a struggle to maintain this sharp focus. So Bradshaw for example would say that we are called as the Church to pray, as the royal priesthood participating in the prayer of Christ, offering a sacrifice of praise and intercession for all.[12] In other words the focus is on what we can do and offer. Contrast this with Packer who regrets that modern

---

[10] Don Carson, 'The Pastor and Worship' in Melvin Tinker (ed.), *The Renewed Pastor* (Fearn: Christian Focus, 2011) p 124.
[11] Gregory Woolfenden, *Daily Liturgical Prayer: Origins and Theology* (Farnham: Ashgate Publishing, 2004) p 294.
[12] Paul Bradshaw, *Reconstructing Early Christian Worship* (London: SPCK, 2009) p 116.

liturgical discussion rarely stresses the principle that services should have a didactic quality and insists that Christian worship is essentially a response to the gospel. He asserts that Cranmer consciously had a structural principle within the *Book of Common Prayer* which gives the services the shape of the gospel of grace through the themes of our need, God's mercy, and our response.[13]

Evelyn Underhill's book *Worship* is often seen as a classic, yet her understanding of the Church of England leads her into classic confusion as she seeks to synthesise the two fundamental theologies mentioned above. She is ready to say that even the 1549 Prayer Book makes plain that 'the English mind is always inclined to assume that a primary object of ordered worship is the edifying of the congregation'[14] and will further assert that this spiritual temper did not spring into existence at the Reformation. Yet she will then go on to laud the great Tractarians for beginning again within the English Church the life of sacrificial worship (by which she means the restoration of a symbolic and sacramental cultus). And so her basic position is that although the *Book of Common Prayer* has lost something through simplification, 'the general sense of the Daily Offices and Eucharist, as we find them in that book, is that of an offering of all life for the service and glory of God'[15]. We have seen already that of course the Christian life is to be viewed as a response of one's entire being to Christ, but Christian gatherings are not primarily for the purpose of making such an offering.

The Reformation disagreements over the purpose of Christian gatherings may appear to belong to a different age, and Underhill's understanding of 'worship' certainly belongs to a different generation. Nevertheless the confusion over why we meet today as Christians persists. When the Liturgical Commission wrote its report 'Transforming Worship' in 2007 we should note the way it defines 'worship' and 'liturgy':

If worship is the deepest response of redeemed humankind to

---

[13] James I Packer, *Tomorrow's Worship* (London: Church Book Room Press, 1966) pp 11-13.
[14] Evelyn Underhill, *Worship* (Cambridge: James Clarke, 2010) p 318.
[15] Ibid., p 315.

God's loving purpose, then liturgy is the set of particular structured actions in which worship is expressed and by which worship is released.[16]

Thus Christian meetings are viewed as an occasion in which our worship of God is to be released and expressed. Although there is some recognition in this report that our worship is a response to what God has done (as indeed is found in any 'offering' view of meetings) the movement from God to man is downplayed. In fact this report seems to have been considerably influenced by developments from within the charismatic movement.

An early exposition of the charismatic movement's understanding of the purpose of Christian meetings is found in Graham Kendrick's book *Worship*. He says for example 'when we gather we can expect to be led into an experience of God's living presence right in the centre of our meeting'.[17] Now we should certainly expect to encounter God when we gather for a Christian meeting but Kendrick appears to focus on music and singing as the key to this. He may acknowledge that it is through faith in Jesus that we meet God the Father and that our worship needs to be informed by the word of God but he says that the principles of Old Testament tabernacle worship are there to instruct us. This can lead him to say for example that 'too often our worship stops short of entering the inner sanctuary'[18] and (in the section headed 'Leading Worship') that the 'task of leading people into the presence of God is a high honour'.[19]

This understanding is in fact typical of what Webber calls the 'Praise and Worship Movement'. He describes what he calls the 'Temple Sequence' in which the worship leader moves the congregation through various steps within the order of service which lead people into the Holy of Holies, and describes some variations on

---

[16] *Transforming Worship: Living the New Creation* (London: General Synod Liturgical Commission, 2007) p 1.
[17] Graham Kendrick, *Worship* (Eastbourne: Kingsway, 1984) p 144.
[18] Ibid., p 149.
[19] Ibid., p 153.

this in the Vineyard movement.[20] Carson points out the dangers of this understanding when he states that it is not worship that leads us into the presence of God, but the death and resurrection of Jesus.[21] Such a charismatic understanding of the purpose of meetings needs to have a sense of historical perspective in which it should be realised that many Christians for centuries (including Anglican Christians using the *Book of Common Prayer*) have come together in meetings in which there has been no singing whatsoever. Are we to conclude from this that these meetings were not really Christian ones after all?

However it is worth noting that when one digs down beneath the vocabulary used there may well be a growing recognition within these circles of the sort of principles that Cranmer used in producing Morning and Evening Prayer. For example, Webber is willing to speak of proclaiming Jesus Christ and his saving reality again and again in worship[22] and Chappell directs our attention to the primary purpose of our gathering as being to re-present and respond to the great story of God's redemption in Christ.[23] This terminology can be misleading because re-presentation of the gospel begs the question as to how that is to be done. Many will not see that re-presentation in terms of the verbal proclamation of the Word of God. Nevertheless the basic idea of responding to the gospel of Christ when we meet together is much more in line with the biblical understanding of worship as expounded by Peterson[24] for example.

The aim of this booklet is to show that a proper understanding of the principles which Cranmer used in producing the *Book of Common Prayer* will bring clarity to the confusion that surrounds the practice of Christians meeting together today. We do not have to use the 1662 *Book of Common Prayer* in order to do this,

---

[20] Robert Webber, *Worship Old and New* (Grand Rapids: Zondervan, 1994) pp 130-131.
[21] Carson, 'The Pastor and Worship' in Tinker (ed) *The Renewed Pastor* p 125.
[22] Webber p 67.
[23] Bryan Chapell, *Christ-Centred Worship* (Grand Rapids: Baker Academic, 2009) pp 116-124.
[24] Peterson, *Engaging with God* pp 283-288.

but we do need to learn from it and acknowledge in our practice how it remains determinative for our Anglican identity.

To that end we will need to review the evidence of what happened when Christians met together in the early centuries of the Church. However, perhaps even more importantly, we will need to make some assessment of how we should use that evidence, in particular whether it is essential that this material shapes our practice today.

We will then survey what Cranmer actually did when undertaking the reform which produced his services of Morning and Evening Prayer, and especially pay regard to the principles which governed his work. We will also need to review how these services fared in the century or so leading up to the production of the 1662 version of the *Book of Common Prayer*.

The outcome of the process of revision of this material during the course of the 20th century may then be assessed in the light of its faithfulness to Cranmer's biblical principles of reform. This will then allow us to consider the question of our practice today, not only in the Church of England but across the Anglican Communion, and indeed the wider Christian scene.

2. Meetings in the early and medieval church and their relevance

In the 20th century the revision of the *Book of Common Prayer* generally took place on historical grounds. In other words it has been considered axiomatic that our present day practice should be shaped by that of the early church. By 'early church' is not meant the apostolic church of the New Testament but the church of the first 500 years or so. Although this principle has been key for Anglican revisions of the service of Holy Communion in particular, this has also been significant for discussions about Morning and Evening Prayer.

It needs to be appreciated that Cranmer did not operate with this principle of trying to recover the models of early church practice. Yet because this methodology has been so dominant in liturgical revision we need to assess what has emerged from these studies of early church practice. Even when the limitations of the historical approach are appreciated this has not prevented writers establishing their theological principles from early evidence in order to justify particular practices today.[1] An author can still state in 2004 that in order to reform daily prayer services one must return to first principles and this involves learning 'from the ancient and medieval sources the principles and the theology that might allow for a fresh start'.[2] That such a statement can be made after over a century of extensive inquiry into ancient sources ought to alert us to the problems with this method of working and should prompt a reconsideration of the very different principles which Cranmer used in his reform. 'First principles' for Cranmer was not about re-establishing primitive practice. He was concerned to reform existing practice in line with the Bible which spoke of the gospel of justification by faith alone in Christ alone.

---

[1] Paul Bradshaw, 'Daily Prayer' in K Stevenson and B Spinks (eds.), *Identity of Anglican Worship* (London: Mowbray, 1991) p 69.
[2] Woolfenden p 294.

Even if one does wish to use ancient historical practice rather than apostolic practice to shape that of the present day, there is a fundamental problem. The basic problem with the methodology of either looking directly for historical material to shape present day practice or establishing theological principles for liturgical revision from this material is the paucity of evidence. The available evidence, especially in the early Christian centuries prior to the Emperor Constantine in the 4th century AD, is too limited to be used safely for these purposes. Little allowance is made for variety of practice in different regions of the Roman Empire, and perhaps even more seriously there is no means of assessing whether the evidence one does have is typical of general practice. Arrangements for Christian meetings in a large city may not be at all representative of what took place in more ordinary gatherings elsewhere.

Having stated this cautionary note about basic methodology it is nonetheless important to survey how church practice did develop. This is important because to understand modern revisions to Morning and Evening Prayer, this forms such a significant background. It is also important because early and medieval practice was what Cranmer was reforming in the 16th century.

References to Christian gatherings in the New Testament remind us that these took place within the context of established Jewish practices. Until 70 AD Jewish practice focussed on three centres – the Temple, the Synagogue and the Home. Beckwith states that Christian worship reforms and develops Jewish worship in accordance with the teaching of Jesus and his saving work.[3] Thus it should not surprise us to find Peter and John going up to the Temple at the time of prayer (Acts 3:1) and references to Stephen having links with the Synagogue of Freedmen (Acts 6:9).

At first sight it may seem relatively straightforward to trace the links between early Christian practices and their Jewish background. However the picture is complicated by the fact that after the destruction of the Temple in 70 AD the strong links between

---

[3] Roger T Beckwith, *Daily and Weekly Worship: Jewish to Christian* (Bramcote: Grove, 1987) p 5.

Christians and this Jewish background were cut. The period in which direct contact existed and influenced Christian practice was therefore only about 40 years. Beckwith further highlights the reality that there were different groupings within 1st century Judaism and that both Jewish and early Christian liturgical texts were rather more variable than they became later on.[4]

Nevertheless it is not difficult to see that Jewish synagogues were places where the reading and exposition of Scripture as well as corporate prayer were key activities. Jesus himself participated in these meetings during his ministry. There is some evidence for the time of prayer being associated with sacrifices in the Temple, for example the daily morning and evening sacrifices. If Christians were not welcome in a synagogue then they could form their own synagogue where they could listen and pray in accordance with the Christian gospel. At home their practices could carry on. In due course the transfer of the day of gathering from the Sabbath to the Lord's Day would have accentuated the separate development of Christian assemblies.

In the evidence from early Christian texts Beckwith asserts that the expectation would be that the Scriptures were read and expounded on Sunday mornings just as they were on Sabbath mornings amongst the Jews. He says that there are few practices of the early church that are better attested than this.[5]

Taft is sceptical about the evidence because he says that no two authors seem to agree about the basics of Jewish worship in the time of Christ.[6] He would be of the opinion that beyond generalisations about Jewish and Christian practice, there is only speculation. Yet even he acknowledges how the New Testament implies that Christians had psalms, hymns, readings and prayer

---

[4] Ibid., p 6.
[5] Ibid., p 25. For example according to Justin Martyr in the mid 2nd century AD Christian Scriptures can be read as an alternative to Jewish Scriptures.
[6] Robert Taft, *The Liturgy of the Hours in East and West: The Origin of the Divine Office and its meaning for today* (Collegeville, Minnesota: Liturgical Press, 1986) p 3.

when they met. He is also content with saying that Christians, like Jews, had the custom of praying at fixed times and that the most important times were the beginning and the end of the day. Rightly he points out though that these times of prayer are natural in any tradition because of the sheer practicality of working hours and so on.

In fact Taft, like so many liturgical writers investigating early church practices regarding non-Eucharistic services, is mainly concerned with tracing the development of what came to be known as the Daily Office. This refers to the public celebration of daily hours of prayer in churches which is found after the time of Constantine (4th century AD), and is ultimately the heritage which Cranmer reformed. It is the attempt to match Christian hours of prayer in this sense to Jewish ones that proves so elusive. This is why in the end Taft says that the evidence in the pre-Constantinian church is so diverse that it excludes facile attempts to harmonise it all.[7]

Burtchaell would also stress the paucity of Christian writings that can be used to determine Christian practice in the period before Constantine in the 4th century AD. Interestingly he argues that when Christians no longer went to synagogue meetings, they brought the pattern of those meetings (readings, preaching, discussion and prayer) into their homes and amalgamated this with the domestic meal. In the Christian community this domestic meeting ultimately became a full assembly of believers (while still meeting in homes since no public assembly would have been allowed). This then became definitively separated from Jewish assemblies as the meetings were transferred from the Sabbath to Sunday.[8]

For the period after Constantine it has been customary to make a distinction between the prayer services held in large churches and those in Christian communities who gathered in the desert to pursue a stricter standard of discipleship. These different patterns of prayer are usually called the cathedral and the monastic offices. In terms of the material available this is a fair distinction so long as it is

---

[7] Ibid., p 27.
[8] James T Burtchaell, *From Synagogue to Church: Public Services and Offices in the earliest Christian communities* (Cambridge: University Press, 1992) p 285.

not regarded as hard and fast. For example Bradshaw argues that in the end the practice of the desert ascetics came to influence some groups of Christians who were to be found in an urban environment.[9]

Bradshaw would say that the intention within the cathedral office was for the Christian community to engage in its priestly task of offering praise and thanksgiving to God on behalf of creation and interceding for the salvation of the world. This is in contrast to the monastic office where the focus was more on personal spiritual development.[10] However, it must be stressed that in both so called cathedral and monastic communities, the available texts are describing a daily pattern of meetings for prayer. It is amongst these Christians that the practice of saying the psalms developed. Yet it was only in larger cities and in desert communities that the practice of this daily office was feasible. It is much more difficult to discern what went on in smaller churches on the Lord's Day and indeed how this daily pattern of praying related to what happened on Sundays.

Scholars argue about the different elements of the cathedral and monastic offices and how they contributed to the pattern of services that emerged in the middle ages. Taft asserts that in Western Europe the practice of Christianity centred round larger churches such as cathedrals and minsters. In these churches there were sufficient clergy to celebrate the daily pattern of services.[11] Out of traditions such as the Benedictines there developed a system of elaborate worship with seven daily offices (Lauds and Vespers were the main services).[12]

However, as the parish church network developed, this elaborate system had to be adapted for more local or itinerant use. The practicalities of this situation meant that it became common for local clergy or friars to fulfil their obligation to keep the daily pattern of prayers by using books which they could take with them. They

---

[9] Bradshaw, *Reconstructing Early Christian Worship*, p 113.
[10] Ibid., pp 105, 110.
[11] Taft, p 297.
[12] Kenneth Stevenson, 'Worship by the Book' in C Hefling and C Shattuck (eds) *Oxford Guide to the Book of Common Prayer* (Oxford: OUP, 2006) p 13.

would thus use a Portifory (carried) or Breviary (shortened) book to do this. Furthermore educated lay people began to use these books of prayers for their own devotional use. These books were known as Books of Hours (or Primers), the hours being a reference to the forms of prayer appropriate for different parts of the day. Cranmer adapted this type of material to create the elements of Morning and Evening Prayer in his *Book of Common Prayer*.[13]

We started this chapter by questioning the methodology which assumes that the practice of the early and medieval church should shape our Christian meetings today. This brief survey of the evidence for early and medieval church practice should have demonstrated the risks involved in doing this. The evidence is too fragmentary and varied to be helpful, even if we wished to base our present practice on the early church rather than the apostles. The difficulties that Christians had in adapting monastic type patterns of prayer for ordinary believers and churches highlights the folly of trying to make the daily offices of either the cathedral or monastic traditions the basis for our Sunday meetings today. Far better then to do what Cranmer did, which was to take these existing patterns of prayer and rigorously shape them to achieve his particular, biblical goals for church meetings. These were certainly not intended primarily to offer praise to God and to intercede for the world.

---

[13] Ibid., p 14.

3. Cranmer's Reform

Bradshaw provides a telling quote from Luther's *Table Talk* which shows the burdensome nature of the recital of the daily office. Luther describes how his busy duties meant that he often found himself weeks behind on the appointed prayers. He says that he would then

> take a Saturday off, or shut myself in for as long as three days without food or drink, until I had said the prescribed prayers. This made my head split, and as a consequence I couldn't close my eyes for five nights, lay sick unto death, and went out of my senses.

When Luther fell three months behind he gave up altogether.[1]

Yet it was on the basis of this type of material that Cranmer worked to produce what we know as Morning and Evening Prayer in the *Book of Common Prayer*. Cranmer and the English reformers laboured to deal with error and superstition but

> held steadily by their purpose to break as little as possible with the worship of the past, and to preserve all that was scriptural and helpful in the older forms of devotion.[2]

It is essential to appreciate that this was the governing principle of the Archbishop's method of reform. Beckwith points out how Cranmer was following Luther in this principle of reforming by stages and in not making greater changes than he could help.[3] A vivid picture of the process by which Cranmer did this is to be found in the biography by MacCulloch.[4]

---

[1] Paul Bradshaw and Simon Jones, 'Daily Prayer' in Paul Bradshaw (ed) *A Companion to Common Worship Volume 2* (London: SPCK, 2006) p 6.

[2] TW Drury and RT Beckwith, *How we got our Prayer Book* (Oxford: Latimer Study 22, 1986) p 4.

[3] Roger Beckwith, 'Thomas Cranmer and the Prayer Book' in Cheslyn Jones, Geoffrey Wainwright, Edward Yarnold (eds.), *The Study of Liturgy* (London: SPCK, 1978) p 70.

[4] Diarmaid MacCulloch, *Thomas Cranmer* (London: Yale, 1996).

After Cranmer became Archbishop in 1532 his first attempts at reform of the daily office were made in the late 1530s. Cranmer was aware of various attempts at reforming the Breviary which were in existence but he was influenced by one in particular: that published by Cardinal Quinones in 1535. Quinones had set about simplifying the Breviary and so the attraction of this work to Cranmer was that in it he had essentially reduced the office to the recitation of the Psalter and the reading of Scripture.[5]

Cranmer devised two schemes to reform the Breviary. The earlier one dated by MacCulloch to perhaps 1538 is actually the more radical.[6] The later one is more conservative because of the political climate later on in Henry VIII's reign. However for our purposes in understanding the principles on which Cranmer operated, the most significant feature of the early scheme is to be found in the preface. Cranmer's preface was itself an adaptation of an introduction by Quinones, and the preface to this early scheme of Cranmer actually found its way, with a few modifications into the preface of the Prayer Book of 1549. This in turn became the Preface of the 1552 book and then the introductory piece entitled 'Concerning the Service of the Church' in 1662. The opening phrase of the latter 'There was never any thing by the wit of man so well devised...' is thus traced back to 1552 and 1549, and then the scheme of 1538 and is in fact ultimately from Quinones.

Nevertheless the key matter to note is the concerns expressed by Cranmer in the preface to his 1538 scheme which is carried on into the 1549 book.[7] His chief concern is that God's Word be heard daily, and alongside this he seeks a single 'use' (as opposed to the variety of schemes that came from Salisbury (the famous 'Sarum Rite'), Hereford, Bangor etc). The nature of the reform needed in order to achieve this goal of hearing God's Word must be appreciated because

---

[5] JD Crichton, 'The Office in the West: The Roman Rite from the Sixteenth Century' in Cheslyn Jones, Geoffrey Wainwright, Edward Yarnold (eds.), *The Study of Liturgy* (London: SPCK, 1978) p 383.

[6] MacCulloch p 222.

[7] See Geoffrey Cuming, *The Godly Order* (London: SPCK 1983) pp 8-13 for the texts of these two prefaces.

it is still of the greatest relevance to our meetings as Christians today. Cranmer said that he had set out a calendar 'having this one object chiefly in view, that the thread and order of holy Scripture shall be continued entire and unbroken'.[8] Cranmer was objecting to the way in which saints' days and other special occasions interrupted the steady voice of God's Word. And the commitment expressed above to the thread and order of Scripture also shows how he saw the Bible as a book with a unified message rather than one in which one might find a few interesting thoughts scattered within it.[9] To recognise this principle in our Christian meetings today would still enormously improve their benefit to those present.

Parallel to Cranmer's efforts at reforming the Breviary to produce services in which God's word could be heard in its entirety, were wider designs to get an English version of the Bible placed in churches. With the encouragement of Cranmer, Thomas Cromwell obtained permission to publish a suitable English version of the Bible in 1538. The resulting *Great Bible* appeared in its first edition in 1539 and with a preface written by Cranmer in the second edition of 1540. In the early years of the Prayer Book of the Church of England this would have been the form in which the voice of God was heard in English churches.[10]

Within the actual scheme to reform the Daily Office which Cranmer devised in 1538 we furthermore see how Cranmer already had in mind the use of this reformed Breviary (if one may call it that) among ordinary (i.e. non monastic) clergy and that he has reduced the eightfold offices of Western monasticism to just two: mattins and vespers (which are of course Morning and Evening Prayer).[11]

---

[8] Cuming, p 10.
[9] This is also noted by John Richardson, 'Have we an Anchor? - Reasserting the Doctrinal Role of the Book of Common Prayer' in *Faith and Worship*, Easter 2011, (Prayer Book Society) p 9.
[10] Gerald Bray, *Translating the Bible* (London: Latimer Trust, 2010) gives the background on pp9-10 as well as Cranmer's preface to the *Great Bible* on pp79-91. See also MacCulloch pp 258-260.
[11] MacCulloch, p 223.

Given the circumstances in which Cranmer was working at the time, this proposal for reform was produced in Latin. However the Archbishop most certainly did have a concern for the laity in mind at this stage[12] and for this to be taken further it was essential that patterns of prayer be developed which were in English. The relevant political opportunity arose for this step in 1544. The Litany was originally a service designed to be used in processions and therefore associated with the veneration of saints. Cranmer produced an English version of this but in doing so he made sure there was no possibility of it being used to worship saints. In a slightly modified form this Litany survives to this day within the 1662 *Book of Common Prayer*. Of particular interest in understanding Cranmer and his principles is the introduction to the Litany entitled 'An Exhortation to Prayer'.[13] This was intended to be read as a sort of homily before the Litany was said. It speaks for example about the foundation of God's word which lies at the basis of the gathering to pray, and it states that it is essential to know what sort of things we should be asking for and the manner in which our prayers should be made. Again that would be sound advice for any Christians who gather to pray nowadays.

One further project relevant to the subject of praying in English was accomplished with Cranmer's involvement prior to the death of King Henry in 1547. This was the publication of the *King's Primer* in 1545. By the 1530s, Primers were used extensively for personal devotional use amongst those who could afford them and read them. The publication of the *King's Primer* was intended to provide uniformity in place of this diversity. The prayers within this book were from a variety of sources. The significance of this for the future was that the text of the *Te Deum, Magnificat*, Lord's Prayer etc found in the *King's Primer* was that which was ultimately used in the *Book of Common Prayer*.

With the arrival of the new King, Edward VI, the project of reformation that had been in gestation for the previous decade could

---

[12] MacCulloch p 224 and this is also evident in the Canon on Shortening Church Prayers for the Preaching of the Word set out in Cuming, p 18.
[13] See W Keatinge Clay, *Private Prayers* (London: Parker Society, 1851) pp 565-576.

now be implemented with greater speed. Much effort was focussed on tackling the service of Holy Communion before the publication of the new Prayer Book in 1549. Within that book Morning and Evening Prayer are of course now in English but the basic scheme is that which Cranmer had been working on around 1538. It then needed to be seen how this Prayer Book worked in practice in ordinary church life. One interesting change from the basic scheme of 1538 that formed the basis for Morning and Evening Prayer in 1549 is that Cranmer put the *Venite* (Psalm 95) back in at the start of Morning Prayer as a special psalm. In 1538 he had left it out apparently considering that it was enough for it to be said in the normal scheme by which the whole psalter was used during the course of a month.[14] Perhaps Cranmer could not resist a special place for a psalm which exhorted its hearers not harden their hearts when they heard God's voice, but he does not appear to have set down the reasons for this change of mind.[15]

Further work of course was done on the service of the Lord's Supper for the 1552 *Book of Common Prayer* which was the next step in Cranmer's project of reformation. However there were also subtle changes made to the services of Morning and Evening Prayer which reflect the realities of how the book was being used in church life.

MacCulloch asserts that Cranmer and others had originally intended the communion service to be the centrepiece of regular Sunday meetings, but that in practice this did not happen. The Morning and Evening Prayer services in 1549 still had the flavour of being intended mainly for the devotional life of the clergy and keen laity, but when the reality of the Prayer Book's use emerged steps were taken in the 1552 book to adapt Mattins and Evensong to these circumstances.[16]

There are various changes which demonstrate that these services were now definitely intended to be attended by a larger congregation. The clergy were told to say these services daily in

---

[14] Cuming, p 16.
[15] Ibid., p 6.
[16] MacCulloch, p 510.

church and to toll the bell so that others would be reminded to attend.[17] Furthermore after the Lord's Prayer at the start of the service the opening versicle was changed from 'O Lord, open thou my lips' (1549) to 'O Lord, open thou our lips' (1552). It is also stated that the congregation should join in the saying of the creed.[18]

It is perhaps in this context that we should note the significant introduction in the 1552 book of a time of Confession of Sin at the start of Morning and Evening Prayer. If the main service on a Sunday was not going to be the Lord's Supper in which the bread and the wine speak so eloquently of the gospel then these Prayer services must remind everyone that the basis of the Christian life is the gospel and that we are sinners in need of God's mercy and grace in Christ.

It is important to appreciate here that while Cranmer had begun by using works culled from a variety of sources, including Lutheran ones and early Christian texts[19], in furthering his reform of the liturgy he was very conscious of the way the Church of England was part of the wider continental reformation. The proposals for the 1552 book were therefore submitted to Martin Bucer and Peter Martyr for their comments. Those of Peter Martyr do not survive but the Censura of Bucer (which consists of these comments) does.

These comments by Bucer immediately inform us of the purpose of church meetings, when Bucer begins by rehearsing his terms of reference which are 'whether I consider there is anything in it which might be more fully explained, in a manner consistent with the word of God and suitable for edification of faith'.[20] As far as

---

[17] Geoffrey Cuming, 'The Office in the Church of England' in Cheslyn Jones, Geoffrey Wainwright, Edward Yarnold (eds.), *The Study of Liturgy* (London: SPCK, 1978) p 394.
[18] The Prayer Books of 1549 and 1552 are conveniently published together in an Everyman's Library edition of 1910 which was republished by the Prayer Book Society in 1999. MacCulloch makes the points about the change in the versicles and the instruction on the creed on p 510.
[19] See for example Drury and Beckwith, *How we got our Prayer Book* pp 11-15.
[20] EC Whitaker, *Martin Bucer and the Book of Common Prayer* (London: Alcuin Club Collections, 55, 1974) p 12.

Morning and Evening Prayer are concerned, Bucer has only a few minor comments which are more to do with the practicalities of leading these services than their actual text. We are told by Bucer that the purpose of all the church's observances is the effective building up of faith in Christ. Because of this principle ministers should recite prayers, psalms and readings with the greatest solemnity and devotion, in a clear and expressive voice, and from a point (in the building) from which everything they say can be easily heard by everyone present. By these means, he concludes, faith will be effectively renewed.[21] It is notable in fact that in correspondence between Peter Martyr and Bucer, on the subject of the 'Reformation of the Rituals', the former is more concerned ultimately about the establishment of doctrine and discipline among the people than 'subjects of smaller importance'.[22] In the practice of our Christian meetings today we too need to remember that their details must not occupy an inordinate amount of time in comparison with this wider picture.

Another aspect of the reforms which produced the 1552 Prayer Book should be appreciated. The way Holy Communion was to be conducted meant that the first part of that order of service could be used by itself. This would be known as ante-communion. The Litany from 1544 was also ordered to be said on Sundays too. This leads to the speculation of MacCulloch that a Sunday morning marathon of prayer, scripture reading and praise could thus be created. However it is by no means clear whether in practice churches really did have mattins, the litany and ante-communion along with a sermon on Sunday mornings.[23]

One might also ask what place the exposition of God's Word had in all this. It is all too easy to be so focussed on the text of the Prayer Book that one loses sight of the overall intention of Cranmer. Cranmer wanted people to hear good sermons. And indeed there is a revealing canon in his first scheme (i.e. circa 1538) for reforming the

---

[21] Whitaker, p 14.
[22] GC Gorham, *Gleanings of a few scattered ears* (London: Parker Society,1857) p 232.
[23] MacCulloch, p 511.

practice of the Office which makes it clear that the public prayers should not be said at the expense of preaching. This meant that he allowed some elements of his scheme for church prayers to be left out when necessary. It is worth quoting part of this in full. After stating explicitly that the goal of church prayers is that everything in the Church should be done for edifying, and that this comes about primarily through wise and learned pastors expounding the word of God, he says

> to ensure that the prolixity of our public prayers here instituted by us should not hinder or in any way delay that work of the good shepherds in teaching their flock, we wish it noted and confirmed by this canon, that whenever any speech of exhortation is to be made to the people or preaching done, then the incumbent may leave out *Te Deum*, the Fourth Lesson and the creed *quicunque vult* (that is the Athanasian creed) in those public prayers when the people are present, so that the people, kept too long and wearied by too lengthy reading, should not attend keenly enough, or should not have enough time to hear the preaching of the gospel and the clear showing-forth of the Spirit of Christ.[24]

When investigating Cranmer's presuppositions, Cuming is quite clear that for the Archbishop, 'the spoken word is more important than the word read out'.[25]

MacCulloch speculates that if given the opportunity Cranmer might have moved the Church of England's liturgy to be closer to that employed by Farel and Calvin and other continental reformers but we

---

[24] Cuming, *Godly Order* p 18.
[25] Cuming, *Godly Order* p 67. An echo of this is also to be found in the 1604 canons where we read 'All ministers likewise shall observe the order, rites and ceremonies prescribed in the book of common prayer, as well in reading the Holy Scriptures and saying of prayers, as in administration of the sacraments, without either diminishing in regard of preaching, or in any other respect, or adding anything in the matter or form thereof'. See Gerald Bray (ed), *The Anglican Canons 1529-1947* (Woodbridge: Boydell & Brewer, Church of England Record Society, 1998) p 283.

should nonetheless be in no doubt that the key work had been done and clear principles for the conduct of Christian meetings had already been established by Cranmer.[26]

At this point we may sum up the principles on which Cranmer conducted his reform of existing material in order to produce what we know as Morning and Evening Prayer. Insofar as these are biblical, these are the principles we ought to bear in mind for our church gatherings today.

For Cranmer, the primary purpose of Morning and Evening Prayer was to edify rather than to offer anything to the Lord. This is seen most clearly in two places that have been referred to in the account above and whose text may now be quoted directly in order to appreciate them. The first is when Cranmer gave a brief to reformers like Bucer and Peter Martyr on asking them to review the proposed 1552 Prayer Book.[27] This is what Bucer says:

> Most reverend Father and Lord, it has been indicated to me ... that your most reverend Paternity has asked that I should assess the contents of the book of sacred rites of this kingdom and indicate whether I consider that there is anything in it which might be more fully explained, in a manner consistent with the word of God and suitable for edification in faith.[28]

Bucer picks up this principle later on as the basis for his comments when he says 'The purpose of all the church's observances is the effective building up of faith in Christ'.[29] Bucer also refers to 1 Corinthians 14 in his response at this point.

The second plain statement of Cranmer's goal is seen in the Canon regarding the shortening of church prayers for the preaching of the Word that is found in the scheme for reforming the Breviary which is dated by MacCulloch and Cuming as early as 1538. This proposed Canon begins thus:

---

[26] MacCulloch, p 512.
[27] The evidence for Cranmer having requested these comments is set out in the Introduction to Whitaker's volume.
[28] Whitaker, p 12.
[29] Ibid., p 14.

> Now since in this edition of church prayers, we are aiming primarily at this goal, that all things should be done in the Church (according to Paul's counsel) for the edifying of the Church...[30]

In Cranmer's mind then the primary purpose of Morning and Evening Prayer was edification. This is not to imply of course that Cranmer ignored the significance of the congregation's response to hearing the Word of God, but for him the chief goal was edification.[31]

We must then note that the chief means to this end of the building of faith is hearing Scripture read and if possible preached. This is why the service was to be conducted in English and why there was such a ruthless pruning of those special days which interrupted the thread of the reading of Scripture. Naturally this scheme was dependent on a daily attendance at both Morning and Evening Prayer. Cranmer was perhaps focussed first of all on clergy getting to hear the voice of God in the whole Bible.

Nevertheless it is evident that right from the beginning of his liturgical reforms Cranmer sought ways in which ordinary lay people could also hear the word of God. On Sundays there were set lessons associated with the Communion service which followed the church calendar. It is not clear how Cranmer would have envisaged ordinary people hearing the continuous reading of the Bible if they only attended the church building on Sundays. Nonetheless we can be safe in saying that Cranmer would have endorsed any scheme which enabled the congregation to listen to the word of God on a sequential pattern and that thus gave people an overall picture of the Bible's message, rather than portions used on a rather inconsistent basis.

We must further note that Cranmer regarded the chief means of renewing and building the people's faith as being through a

---

[30] Cuming, p 18.
[31] In writing to Queen Mary in 1555, Cranmer stated why church services should not revert to Latin and says that the various elements of the service must be said in English so that the people's response can be a sweet savour in God's nose. See G Duffield (ed) *The Work of Thomas Cranmer* (Appleford: Sutton Courtenay Press, 1965) pp 291-292.

sermon by a well trained pastor who carefully expounded the word of God. This meant that where this was possible the saying of the full version of the set forms of Morning and Evening Prayer might be shortened. This too is of significance as we seek to apply the admirable and biblical principles of Cranmer to Christian meetings today.

Having said that though, even in congregations where there is a good and competent preaching ministry, the use of an equivalent liturgy to Cranmer's Morning and Evening Prayer should not be neglected today. Packer points out how Cranmer hammered the liturgy into a gospel shape. He remarks that Cranmer was not a liturgical antiquarian but that his aim was to adapt time honoured forms to secure clear expression in Christian meetings of the gospel of justification by faith.[32] Indeed he argues elsewhere that an awareness of the fact of the principle of *lex orandi, lex credendi* is of vast significance. In other words how we pray (in the sense of the content of our Christian meetings) moulds what we believe. In Morning and Evening Prayer there is a consistent pattern of confession of sin, followed by the proclamation of grace in Christ which then calls us to exercise faith in God's Word to us.[33]

Every time we meet as Christians we need to be reminded of the basic elements of the gospel because this is the basis of the Christian life. Even if we are doing a detailed sermon series on, say, the book of Proverbs we all need to be confronted with sin, mercy, and faith as the basis of following Jesus Christ since our sinful nature always seeks to find alternatives to this foundation for our discipleship. This vital principle that it is not only our sermons but

---

[32] James I Packer, *Tomorrow's Worship* p 13.
[33] James I Packer, 'Gain and Loss' in RT Beckwith (ed.) *Towards a Modern Prayer Book* p77, where he asserts that the gospel pattern of the Prayer Book kept the Church of England from suffering the modernist landslide that the Free Churches suffered in the late 19th and early 20th century. For a description of the gospel pattern in Morning and Evening Prayer see Packer 'Gospel in the Prayer Book' on website http://www.stpaulsanglicanchurch.org/gospel_prayer_book.php and Packer *Tomorrow's Worship* p 12.

the rest of our Christian meetings which need to communicate the gospel is recognised by a variety of evangelical writers.[34] If we do not make the effort to communicate the gospel clearly in the entirety of our Christian meetings, then we will end up communicating something else.

---

[34] See Chappell, *Christ-Centred Worship* pp 17-19 and Mark Ashton, 'Following in Cranmer's Footsteps' in D Carson (ed), *Worship by the Book* (Grand Rapids: Zondervan, 2002) pp 64-107. Note especially Ashton's comment on p 74 that Cranmer shows us how to work out biblical doctrine in liturgical practice. The same idea is found in Tony Payne, 'Better church: the why and how of running Sunday meetings' *The Briefing (UK edition)* vol 397 (March/April 2012) pp 13-19.

4. After Cranmer

The *Book of Common Prayer* was banned from use twice in the century or so after the 1552 version. Once was during the reign of Queen Mary when of course Archbishop Cranmer himself was martyred, and the other was during the Commonwealth period. These periods when its use was outlawed to some extent, reflect the two most important pressures which were brought to bear on the *Book of Common Prayer* in order to divert it from the practice of Christianity that it was seeking to inculcate. Since both pressures still continue to bear down on Cranmer's biblical principles for the conduct of Christian meetings we will need to examine each of these in turn and observe how the Prayer Book then emerged in 1662. Under Mary the Prayer Book was banned because it inculcated the gospel of justification by faith in Christ alone in a powerful way. It was banned under the Commonwealth because it was naively thought better to trust ministers to conduct Christian meetings through general points of guidance rather than through any set form of words.

When Protestant Christianity was re-established after the death of Queen Mary in 1558 many who had been exiled elsewhere in Europe returned to England. These men, who had experienced other situations and circumstances, were naturally part of the leadership of the Church of England as it sought to establish and consolidate the work of Reformation so that the whole nation might hear the gospel and be edified through the teaching and preaching of the Bible.

As this work was undertaken disagreements about the best way to reform the church emerged, and inevitably perhaps the Prayer Book provided a focus for some of these disagreements. A proper understanding of the nature of the issues has been bedevilled by a simplistic use of the word 'Puritan'. Writing over 40 years ago Horton Davies could say that theological differences between Anglicanism and Puritanism led to differences in the practice of worship.[1] In fact we need to recognise that the word 'Anglicanism' was not employed until the early 19th century and that it was only a minority of those people who were known as Puritans that disagreed strongly with the Church of England's practice of Christianity as set out in the *Book of Common Prayer*. Collinson says that prejudice against human set forms of prayer may have been representative of the separatists, but that it does not convey the attitude and practice of Puritans properly so called, who remained within the establishment.[2]

One particular episode, known as the Admonition Controversy, which took place in the 1570s highlighted the real nature of the tensions and disagreements within the leadership of the Church of England as ministers strove to establish the work of the gospel in England. Andrew Cinnamond describes how resentment at the position which Queen Elizabeth had taken on further reform led to frustration amongst some clergy.[3] Out of these Puritan frustrations emerged the 1572 Admonition to Parliament which was written by two London clergy called Thomas Wilcox and John Field. Frere and Douglas see this as the first open manifesto of the Puritan party and the point at which Puritanism began to be regarded as a hostile force.[4] Cinnamond points out that as in so many views of Puritanism it is readily seen as hostile and a foreign import, yet in fact the arguments set out by Wilcox and Field were not new. He also states that some older Puritans were shocked by the tone of the Admonition and that it was at this point that Puritanism began to be associated with the implementation of a presbyterian form of church government. Only after this was dealt with in a crackdown in the 1590s was Puritanism able to free itself from that association.

---

[1] Horton Davies, *Worship and Theology in England: Volume 2 From Cranmer to Hooker 1534-1603* (Princeton: Princeton University Press, 1970) p 69.

[2] Patrick Collinson, *The Elizabethan Puritan Movement* (Oxford: Clarendon Press, 1990) p 356.

[3] Andrew Cinnamond, *What matters in reforming the Church? Puritan Grievances under Elizabeth I* (London: Latimer Trust, St Antholin Lecture 2011) p 7.

[4] WH Frere and CE Douglas (eds.), *Puritan Manifestoes: A Study of the Origin of the Puritan Revolt* (London: SPCK, 1907).

The Admonition Controversy ran between 1572 and 1577. John Whitgift (then Dean of Lincoln and later Archbishop of Canterbury) was chosen to respond to the initial Admonition, but later on the controversy was essentially between Whitgift and Thomas Cartwright. There was personal history between these two men which did not help calm the tone of debate. The essence of the argument, at least insofar as it focussed on the conduct of Christian meetings, is expressed in the famous phrase which dismissed the Prayer Book as 'an unperfect book, culled and picked out of the popish dunghill'. This vivid condemnation is more soberly expressed by Cartwright who states that 'the whole liturgy and public service of the Church of England' is 'taken from the church of antichrist'.[5] We may observe immediately that this is in reality an assault on Cranmer's principle of taking existing material and ruthlessly reworking it so as to make it biblical.

Although some of the points of the controversy appear to centre on matters such as the use of the signing of the cross in baptism and the ring in the marriage ceremony, it is the association of these practices with the Roman Catholic church that so disturbs Cartwright and those who followed his line. Thus in the face of continued low spiritual standards among English people, Cartwright and his party are essentially saying that the key to sorting this out is to remove all traces of any association with Roman Catholic practice from the Church of England. However Whitgift and conformists like him see the *Book of Common Prayer* as a powerful way of promulgating Protestant doctrine and have great confidence in the restorative effect of good teaching.[6] We can see a similar process at work in Cartwright's commitment to a presbyterian form of church government (in which bishops of course are done away with). It is seen, mistakenly, as the key to improving spiritual standards. Those like Whitgift who resisted this knew that improving spiritual standards depended to a far greater extent on the quality of ministers.

---

[5] Andrew Cinnamond, *Diversity in the English Reformed Tradition: An Introduction to the Admonition Controversy* (Unpublished PhD thesis, 2011) p 152.
[6] Ibid., pp 153-154, 158.

Collinson perceptively sees what is really going on in the way that some of these arguments are interpreted today. He says that we must not look at the worship of 16th century Calvinists through the spectacles of the modern liturgical movement. For Elizabethan Puritans the liturgical part of the service was always subordinate to the ministry of the Word. He notes that one of the more serious objections to the Prayer Book was that it reversed these priorities.[7] Yet we have already seen in our assessment of Cranmer's work on Morning and Evening Prayer that he certainly did not reverse those priorities. Those who objected to the Prayer Book on such grounds did not understand Cranmer or were merely objecting to the way in which many clergy actually conducted meetings using the Prayer Book. Given Collinson's observation above about the modern liturgical movement it is then surprising to find him saying that the heart of puritan worship was directed to a definite end that differed radically from medieval and Anglican worship which dwelt richly upon devotion for its own sake.[8] This is hardly consistent with the Cranmer who so determinedly made Morning and Evening Prayer times when God's voice was to be heard and the basic elements of the gospel impressed upon the congregation. To say that puritan worship has a different aim from Anglican worship depends on whether you take Cranmer seriously in defining the nature of Anglican worship.

Naturally it needs to be recognised that it is one thing to set out ideals in terms of the use of the Prayer Book in ordinary parish life, but it is quite another to ascertain what actually happened. Judith Maltby has attempted to discern something of the actual practice of the Prayer Book and conformity to it in the period from the Reformation to the outbreak of the Civil War.[9] In the face of a focus in historical studies on Puritan complaints about the Prayer Book she

---

[7] Collinson, *The Elizabethan Puritan Movement* p 358.
[8] Ibid., p 358.
[9] Judith Maltby, *Prayer Book and People in Elizabethan and Early Stuart England* (Cambridge: University Press, 1998).

shows that there was a significant body of lay people who developed a considerable attachment to the Prayer Book.[10]

Maltby bases her work on evidence from church courts in which the laity complain about the behaviour of their ministers. Naturally a focus on such evidence will tend to highlight the cases where the relationship between pastor and people has broken down, and she warns that it is not always possible to discern whether the clergy are cited for a failure to conform to the requirements of the Prayer Book or for sheer negligence. In the end though, Maltby's evidence demonstrates some validity to the complaints of certain Puritans about the poor standards of ministry among the clergy. This would substantiate the complaint in the Admonition of 1572 that 'there is no edification according to the rule of the Apostle, but confusion'.[11] Yet the court evidence also demonstrates cases of the zeal and concern by people to have their (Prayer Book) Sunday services as was their due.[12]

Ultimately the politicisation of the Puritan spiritual movement led to radical developments under the Commonwealth in which the Prayer Book was banned. In its place the Westminster Assembly authorised its *Directory* in 1644. This reflected the efforts of the previous 100 years to reform the *Book of Common Prayer* and was heavily influenced by Scottish presbyterians and English independents.[13] Positively, Breward notes that the Westminster *Directory* provided a framework for serious puritan piety in which worship grew out of thankful and obedient response to Scripture. However he says that the authors of this *Directory* did not appreciate

---

[10] Maltby, *Prayer Book and People in Elizabethan and Early Stuart England* pp 229-230.

[11] Ibid., p 36.

[12] Note also the way she surveys this evidence and remarks that the Laudian agenda was unpopular with Prayer Book Protestants as well as Puritans. See Judith Maltby, 'The Prayer Book and the Parish Church: From the Elizabethan Settlement to the Restoration', in C Hefling and C Shattuck (eds.), *The Oxford Guide to the Book of Common Prayer* (Oxford: OUP, 2006) pp 79-92.

[13] Ian Breward, Introduction, in *The Westminster Directory* (Bramcote: Grove Liturgical Study 21, 1980) p 4.

how rapidly moralism would undermine its desire to deal with ignorance and superstition. Breward believes that it was a notable attempt to combine order and freedom in faithfulness to Scripture alone but that in fact it was only appropriate for a covenanted minority since it was too demanding for a folk church. It was too minister centred to carry the gospel in good times and in bad.[14]

The Preface to the *Directory* gives the reasons for abandoning the *Book of Common Prayer* and the reasons for laying aside its Liturgy and replacing it with a Directory.[15] It is worth noting some of these as we continue to hear echoes of them to this day. The preface states that despite the good intention of the compilers of the Prayer Book, long experience has shown it to be an offence to many of the godly at home and also the Reformed Churches abroad. Reading all the prayers in the Prayer Book was seen as burdensome and the Papists also boasted that the Prayer Book fitted with a good deal of their own manner of Service. The Liturgy is also blamed for increasing an idle and unedifying ministry which contented itself with set forms.

All through this period of a hundred years after the 1552 Prayer Book we note Puritan dissatisfaction with the state of the Church of England finding expression in criticism of the *Book of Common Prayer*. It is always tempting to advocate easy solutions to very difficult and deep spiritual problems. Yet when the opportunity appeared to do away with the Prayer Book the reality was that these apparently obvious and straightforward solutions did not achieve what they were supposed to do. There is no avoiding the fact that freer forms of service are enormously dependent on the quality of the minister who leads them. In places where the minister is less than well equipped to preach and lead the meeting, then at least a set liturgy which is biblically based can provide the people with some of the refreshment in the gospel which they need.

The dislike of the Church of England and its practices which was politically expressed under the Commonwealth was also stoked by the rise to power in the Church of those around William Laud

---

[14] Breward, *The Westminster Directory* p 6.
[15] Ibid., pp 8-9.

during the period before the Civil War. Within this group someone like John Cosin provides a representative view of their attitude to the Prayer Book through his Notes upon this. Of course we should be in no doubt that Cosin saw himself as a Protestant[16] yet these notes betray different principles from those of Cranmer, attitudes which were to become much more acceptable from the 19th century onwards in the Church of England. Thus Cosin can say that the solemn beginning of the (Morning Prayer) service shows that all which follows is solemn service of God, and that confession makes our service acceptable to Him, and that the Psalms are a main part of God's public service.[17]

Nevertheless despite the pressure of some Puritans for free forms of prayer and that of Laudians who wanted to interpret Cranmer in a very different sense, the actual changes in the *Book of Common Prayer* between 1552 and 1662 were very few. As far as Morning and Evening Prayer are concerned they are mainly the addition of certain special prayers to be said after the third collect at the end of each service.[18] In 1559 a table of Sunday Lessons was added. This reflected the fact that not enough lay people attended church on weekdays for the daily readings to be continued on Sundays as Cranmer had originally hoped.[19] In 1604 the meaning of the word 'Absolution' in these services was explained by the addition of 'Or Remission of Sins'. In the Litany of 1662 the prayer that God would illuminate all Bishops, Pastors and ministers of the Church was replaced by the petition for the illumination of all Bishops, Priests and Deacons.

It is striking then that after all vicissitudes of the previous century the 1662 Prayer Book really had not changed very much from that set out by Cranmer himself in 1552. That in itself appears to be a

---

[16] Cuming, *The Godly Order* p 129 writes 'But if Cosin was no Puritan, neither was he a Roman Catholic'.
[17] John Cosin, *Works volume 5: Notes and collections on the Book of Common Prayer* (Oxford: JH Parker 1855) pp 442, 448.
[18] These changes may be conveniently consulted in Drury and Beckwith, *How we got our Prayer Book*, pp 32-50.
[19] Drury and Beckwith, *How we got our Prayer Book* p 35.

testimony to the wisdom of the principles by which Cranmer conducted his reform. However although the use of the Prayer Book now entered what has been called a Golden Age,[20] the attachment to Cranmer's principles, even in Morning and Evening Prayer was not to endure the upheavals of the 20th century.

---

[20] Jeremy Gregory, 'The Prayer Book and the Parish Church: From the Restoration to the Oxford Movement', in C Hefling and C Shattuck (eds.), *The Oxford Guide to the Book of Common Prayer*, p 93.

5. The Modern Era

Until the early 19th century and the appearance of the Oxford Movement it is believed that there was broad agreement across the Church of England on the outline and structure of its Sunday services. The most frequent services would have been Morning and Evening Prayer.[1] A significant development after 1662 however was the gradual introduction of hymns.

Within the 19th century the increasing influence of Anglo-Catholic ideas which came through the Oxford Movement, and later on the development of theological liberalism, did little to change the general practice of services in the majority of parishes. Nevertheless Anglo-Catholic and liberal ideas did begin to have a significant impact on parochial practice within the 20th century.

Some of the pressure for changes to the existing *Book of Common Prayer* was entirely understandable. Additional material for new circumstances and the introduction of some flexibility in practice would have commanded widespread support. However the theological developments of the previous century meant that there was also pressure to change the actual doctrine that Church of England services expressed. Anglo-Catholics wished to reverse the Reformation, and liberals wished to loosen the Church's attitude to the Bible. This meant that when the fruit of efforts at revision were set out in the 1928 Prayer Book, it was rejected by Parliament because it fell between two stools. It was not conservative enough for some and too conservative for others.[2]

As far as the future fate of Morning and Evening Prayer services are concerned significant indications of what was to come appear within the 1928 book. In some circumstances the introductory

---

[1] Jeremy Gregory, The Prayer Book and the Parish Church: From the Restoration to the Oxford Movement, *The Oxford Guide to the Book of Common Prayer* pp 93-105.

[2] For an excellent account of this controversy see John Maiden, *Religion and National Identity* (Woodbridge: Boydell, 2009).

confession of sins can be omitted and an alternative expression of the purpose of meeting together begins with the statement

> we are come together in the presence of Almighty God ... to offer unto him through our Lord Jesus Christ our worship and praise and thanksgiving.

Of course it is not that we do not meet together to praise God but the problem arises when this is seen as the chief goal of our gathering. Cranmer in his Exhortation expressed his principle of meeting in order to be edified by firstly stressing the gospel pattern of confession and forgiveness and only then speaking of praise and thanksgiving. He then spoke of hearing God's Word (which is not mentioned at all in the 1928 alternative) and praying.[3]

The rejection of the 1928 Prayer Book unfortunately led to church members getting accustomed to using texts without proper authorisation[4] and thus a more Do it Yourself attitude to the use of the liturgy. However even more significant in the period after 1928, was the rise of the Parish Communion movement. Through this the Anglo-Catholic commitment to having Holy Communion as the main service on Sundays became widespread within the Church of England. Thus by the time of the 1960s when revision of the Prayer Book was in full flood, this had come to be the normal experience of the majority of Church of England parishes (even evangelicals were committed to this according to the statement of the 1967 Keele Congress). During the period of revision, this reality may have influenced the role which Morning and Evening Prayer on Sundays were expected to play.

---

[3] See James Packer's comments on this in 'Gain and Loss', in RT Beckwith (ed.) *Towards a Modern Prayer Book* p 84: 'The aim of the penitential introduction... was to show that Christian praise and prayer spring from the knowledge of the remission of sins'. He also quotes Raymond Abba in saying that 'worship, to be Christian, must embody and set forth before the eyes of the worshipper the great historic facts of the Christian revelation so that the worshipping Church may respond in penitence and thanksgiving, dedication and praise' p 74.

[4] Trevor Lloyd, 'Church of England: Common Worship', in C Hefling and C Shattuck (eds.), *The Oxford Guide to the Book of Common Prayer* p 413.

A key report in the period leading up to the revision work of the 1960s was 'Prayer Book Revision in the Church of England' published in 1958. In the section on guiding principles for future Prayer Book Revision we see an insistence that revision must not represent a radical break with the past. Yet there is also a commitment to expressing the liturgical and theological insights of our time.[5] The significance of this is found when it speaks of the way in which appeal is made to the 1549 Act of Uniformity's reference to the 'usages of the primitive church'. The report then states that studies over the last 30 years have shown what these usages were and that the 16th century Reformers could not have known this. In other words there is here a commitment to be guided by early church practice rather than biblical principles. Cranmer knew very well the difference between the two and Beckwith explains the true sense in which Cranmer used that phrase in 1549.[6]

The *Alternative Service Book* (ASB) of 1980 was the fruit of the period of revision which was especially prominent in the 1960s. Since matters have moved on from the ASB there is little point in pursuing the details of the changes to Morning and Evening Prayer, but it is worth noting some of the principles which undergird these.

Packer highlights the way in which the modern shibboleth of the period that our worship should conform to the primitive church is a liturgical 'By Path Meadow'.[7] He says the ideal of worship is to

---

[5] *Prayer Book Revision in the Church of England* (London: SPCK, 1958) pp 29-30.

[6] Roger Beckwith, 'Alternative Services: Second Series', in RT Beckwith (ed.) *Towards a Modern Prayer Book* p 49. Beckwith says that in the 1549 Act of Uniformity the expression 'usages of the primitive church' is to be understood as relating to the sort of material which is found in the Preface of the 1549 Prayer Book (which became 'Concerning the Service of the Church' in the 1662 Prayer Book), and not as a key principle which guided Cranmer. Cranmer's devotion to antiquity was always in second place to the biblical principle of edification.

[7] A phrase coined in Bunyan's *Pilgrim's Progress* to refer to a wrong turning.

embody the gospel and that no other ideal is biblically defensible.[8] More specifically within the revisions proposed for Morning and Evening Prayer Packer speaks of the way in which the momentousness of our sin and of God's forgiveness is played down. This is witnessed by the way in which the penitential introduction to Morning or Evening Prayer can be omitted.[9] This significant change is indeed ultimately found within the ASB where there are shorter forms of Morning and Evening Prayer, and although the full form (with the penitential introduction) is recommended for use on Sundays, this is not regarded as essential.

Furthermore the form in which the confession is introduced (when the penitential section is used) now entirely reflects the alternative exhortation of the 1928 Prayer Book. In fact it can hardly be called an Exhortation with the purpose of encouraging us to confess our sins because really it is simply an Introduction which explains the purpose of our gathering together. Although in the ASB we can now be glad to find that we are gathering among other things to 'hear and receive his holy word', the purpose of offering God our praise and thanksgiving is now uppermost. The link which Cranmer established between hearing the gospel call to confess our sins and then responding with praise and thanksgiving for God's mercy in Christ has now been broken.

It is not that those who alerted others to the nature of these changes taking place in this period of revision were opposed to all change in the 1662 Book. Packer spoke of the need for conservative

---

[8] Packer *Tomorrow's Worship* pp 28-29. This is also noted by R Beckwith in his comments on the services which the Liturgical Commission produced in 1962. He says that it is proposed that ancient Christian worship rather than the Prayer Book should be the norm of Anglican worship. See Beckwith, Alternative Services: Second Series in RT Beckwith (ed.) *Towards a Modern Prayer Book* pp 46-47.

[9] Packer, Gain and Loss, in *Towards a Modern Prayer Book*, pp 83-83. Beckwith even wonders whether this change has been introduced precisely because the penitential introduction was not added to the daily offices until the Reformation. Beckwith, Alternative Services: Second Series, in *Towards a Modern Prayer Book* p 52.

revision.[10] More specifically he spoke of the need for additional prayers, an adaptation for special services (including presumably the family services that were then being used experimentally) and the promotion of flexibility and variety within the framework of the existing services for example. He wondered whether Evening Prayer needed to be so similar to Morning Prayer, and he felt that the vastly improved levels of literacy allowed for more congregational participation. Often some arguments for change were driven by a focus on the issue of appropriate language, but he points out that unintelligibility can reflect a spiritual as well as a linguistic problem.[11]

Contemporary with the revision activity on the Prayer Book in the 1960s were two other elements in the life of the Church of England. One was the development of Family Services. The other was the appearance of the charismatic movement.

Wilkinson traces the origins of more informal services back to provision in 1872 when it became permissible to hold a third service in addition to Morning and Evening Prayer in which material from the Bible and Prayer Book were used, along with hymns. He is aware however that by the 1960s these limits were unrealistic, and so he seeks to outline the basic principles which underlie such informal services. He notes that these informal services fall into two obvious categories, namely those intended for special occasions and those designed to be used regularly.[12]

Wilkinson reflects on Morning Prayer and Antecommunion in order to propound a four-fold shape to family services: Opening, Office, Prayers, Conclusion. No doubt it is helpful to have a basic structure in mind when preparing informal services, but his exposition of these elements demonstrates a serious divergence from Cranmer's understanding of the purpose of gathering together. Thus within the Opening he says that penitence is only one of a number of suitable reactions to an awareness that God is present and that the *Book of Common Prayer* inherits a medieval emphasis on penitence

---

[10] Packer, *Tomorrow's Worship*, p 30.
[11] Ibid., pp 20-23.
[12] John Wilkinson, *Family & Evangelistic Services* (London: CIO, 1967) pp 7-8.

which would have appeared extreme in the first seven centuries of Christian Prayer. This is entirely at odds with Cranmer's desire to bring us back to the basic gospel pattern of sin, mercy and faith every time we meet, let alone the reality that it was the Archbishop who added in the confession element to Morning and Evening Prayer in 1552!

He shows a greater appreciation of the purpose of what he identifies as the Office in saying that it is designed to bring the people into contact with the Bible and its revelation. Furthermore his awareness that some people find certain parts of the Bible difficult to understand may be commendable, but his proposed solution of perhaps using other books such as those by CS Lewis or D Bonhoeffer as an alternative betrays an attitude far removed from Cranmer's confidence that hearing the Word of God will transform lives through the work of the Holy Spirit.[13]

This understanding of Family Services is significant because it heralds some of the ideas behind the provision of services in *Common Worship* today. *Common Worship* replaced the ASB in the year 2000. Thus Mark Earey includes among the principles behind *Common Worship* services the importance of structure and shape, flexibility and adaptability, and yet the need to try and preserve a family likeness so that local services are connected both to the Church of England and to the wider church.[14] The challenge is how one can do this when there is confusion over the basic reason why we are meeting. Are we meeting primarily to offer something to God or is the chief purpose for our gathering to hear God speak to us?

What is known as the charismatic movement began essentially within the Church of England and other denominations in the 1960s. Initially its impact on Sunday services was found in the use of new songs. These began to be incorporated in many churches alongside traditional hymns. Inevitably many of the new songs did not last, but the general encouragement the movement brought to

---

[13] Wilkinson, pp 16-26.
[14] Mark Earey, *Producing Your Own Orders of Service* (London: Church House Publishing, 2000) p 4.

compose songs in contemporary style has been widely welcomed. Yet alongside this there has developed an understanding of the role of singing in our congregational meetings which is much more problematic. This has been alluded to already in the introduction (pp7-8), but here we need to note that this has come to influence widely the common understanding of why we meet together as Christians. Take for example the definition of liturgy given in 'Transforming Worship':

> If worship is the deepest response of redeemed humankind to God's loving purpose, then liturgy is the set of particular structured actions in which worship is expressed and by which worship is released.[15]

The charismatic movement has been criticised for stressing experience at the expense of biblical content. This is not always true or fair but that criticism can certainly be levelled at the 'Transforming Worship' report. We are told that liturgy is essential to the formation of Christian community, and that the experience of encountering a community engaged in authentic worship is powerfully attractive.[16] Many will read that as saying that it is the reality and authenticity of the experience that is paramount. Authentic experience in Christian gatherings is necessary but it is not sufficient since the meetings of followers of other religions may have a liturgy and they too may have something about them which is powerfully attractive. What makes a meeting authentically Christian is content that is shaped by the gospel message, and a purpose which reflects a biblical understanding of why we gather together. Cranmer's *Book of Common Prayer* expressed these clearly, but *Common Worship* and the practice of many churches today do not necessarily do so.

Common Worship of course provides for the use of a traditional form of Morning and Evening Prayer but this is only one option among many for those services which are not Holy Communion. It has done nothing to deal with the departures from Cranmer's principles which have been promoted within the 20th

---

[15] *Transforming Worship: Living the New Creation* p 1.
[16] *Transforming Worship: Living the New Creation* pp 5-6.

century. The idea of our meeting together primarily to offer our praise to God rather than to hear and respond to God's word predominates. Even the traditional language version of Morning and Evening Prayer, which could give the impression that it is directly from the 1662 Book, in reality allows much of the initial exhortation to confession to be omitted, and also includes the defective 1928 version of the exhortation.

Within the modern language versions of Morning and Evening Prayer we can be thankful to be told that 'Prayers of Penitence are used when Morning/Evening Prayer is the principal service', yet the introduction to this is based on the ASB. We have already given reasons why this cannot be called an exhortation any more (see p.40). There is of course plenty of variety and optional material in *Common Worship*, supremely in what is called the Service of the Word. This at least enables those who wish to have Christian meetings conducted along Cranmerian (and biblical) principles in a flexible way to do so.

The origins of the Service of Word lie in the tradition of family services that had developed since the 1960s. It was proposed in 1989 to allow flexibility and variety and to meet local worship needs. It is explicitly acknowledged as being designed in the form of a Directory (i.e. similar in genre to that used during the Commonwealth period).[17] This means of course that it is highly dependent on the quality of the minister leading the service. If that individual does not have a clear grasp of the principles for Christians gathering together then the result can be painful and destructive.

Overall we have to conclude that *Common Worship* faithfully reflects the current state of the Church of England in its confusion and variety of practice. Perhaps one can say that *lex credendi* is indeed now expressed in *lex orandi*. Even within services which purport to be descended from Cranmer's Morning and Evening Prayer there is a confusion and variety of practice that reflects the confusion about the Christian message within the Church of England today.

---

[17] Lloyd, 'Church of England: Common Worship', in C Hefling and C Shattuck (eds.), *The Oxford Guide to the Book of Common Prayer*, p 414.

6. What Now?

In the face of the confusion of practice over the way we should conduct Christian meetings, a confusion that is found not only in the Church of England but also more widely, we inevitably wonder how we can find a way forward. There is a lot to be said for negotiating the current confusion by referring to the biblical principles of Thomas Cranmer which we find undergirding his Morning and Evening Prayer within the *Book of Common Prayer*.

Perhaps the first principle we should keep before us is that the way we conduct our meetings and the content of them have a profound impact on the congregation. They mould and shape our understanding of the Christian gospel and what it means to be a disciple of Jesus Christ. Cranmer was all too aware that the principle of *lex orandi, lex credendi* is so true, for good or ill. If we do not think carefully and biblically about what we are doing when we meet then we may well find that our meetings are doing more harm than good. If we want our meetings to shape people in living out the Christian gospel, then it is not only the sermon but everything else within our meetings which needs to reflect that intention.

In view of the history outlined in these pages we also need to be aware of false understandings of why we are meeting. If we use terms like 'worship' and 'service' we need to be very careful because Cranmer knew well that the Bible saw Christian meetings as people gathering primarily to hear from God rather than to offer anything to him. Christian meetings form part of the lives of disciples who seek to serve and worship God through their Saviour the Lord Jesus Christ, but it is because we always need to be renewed in making the gospel the basis of our discipleship that we gather primarily to hear God's Word.

Of course the response to that Word will involve praise and singing for example, but that is not the primary purpose of our gathering. According to Cranmer we meet for edification and not for offering. And according to Cranmer God is present with us by the Holy Spirit as his Word is heard. We must not imagine that we enter the presence of the Lord through singing.

We have also seen that Cranmer was happy to adapt existing forms in order to achieve his purpose of edification. This use of earlier forms of the Daily Office has been misunderstood as an endorsement of the idea that ancient liturgical forms should provide the model for our practice today. That is not at all what Cranmer had in mind. In Morning and Evening Prayer Cranmer strove to give expression to biblical principles for the conduct of Christian meetings. Ancient liturgical models are never to be followed for their own sake.

Furthermore we have noted the wisdom of Cranmer's policy of not breaking unnecessarily with the past. When some Puritans sought to order public meetings with greater freedom using a Directory, the limitations of this became apparent. The passing centuries have only reinforced this. Great freedom in the directions for conducting Christian meetings is dependent upon great abilities and insight in the minister and others who lead those meetings.[1]

In meeting then as Christians today, Cranmer's principles can help us reflect the authentic pattern of biblical spirituality. Our priority in meeting is to hear God's Word. This may come to us in a variety of forms, but an awareness of our need to be sustained by the word of life must be paramount. This is the normal means by which the Holy Spirit shapes and moulds our lives so that in the rest of the week we are equipped to please God in our different spheres of service.

Above all in meeting together as the Lord's people we need to be brought face to face with the basic principles of the Christian gospel. We need to be reminded that we are sinners who have no hope apart from the death of Christ. We need to rejoice in the mercy of the Lord in Christ. We need to be encouraged to respond with faith and love to the Lord as he speaks to us from the Scriptures. As we meet together we are to encourage one another to be clear about the gospel and to apply it to our lives. There is no Christian who is

---

[1] It is interesting to note the recent expression of appreciation by a presbyterian for a modest amount of formal liturgical structure. See Carl Trueman, 'A Word to the Conscience', *Themelios* 36.2 (2011) pp 183-184.

mature enough not to need a regular reminder of the Christian message and to grow in it. These are the biblical principles which governed Cranmer's reforms and that led to Morning and Evening Prayer as we have them in the 1662 *Book of Common Prayer*.

We may wish to encourage some variety in the application of those principles to the liturgy we use today but we are betraying the wisdom of many centuries if we lose sight of those principles. Even in the 1960s when the process of Prayer Book revision reached its apogee, evangelicals did not urge a rigid retention of the 1662 Book, but rather argued for a modest reform in which Cranmer's principles were retained. Of course the different provinces of the Anglican Communion have produced their own Prayer Books too. These tend to be derived above all from the 1662 Book but again many have also emulated unhelpful developments within the Church of England. A re-acquaintance with Cranmer's principles would thus serve the Anglican Communion more generally, even if the particular application of them in the different provinces might vary.

There remain some particular issues which we face today that are worth considering in the light of these biblical principles which Cranmer employed. We should not think for example that the ready availability of Bibles nowadays means that they are read regularly, even by those who attend church consistently. In the busyness of work and home, we need to recognise that for many their only exposure to the voice of God will actually be when they come to church meetings.

Thus it may be that the modern evangelical practice of simply having a short passage of the Bible read which then provides the basis for an expository sermon is not enough. Many will feel that it is not appropriate to use the particular system of Bible readings known as the *Common Worship* lectionary though. Modern lectionaries have tended to regress from Cranmer's aims so that the continuous reading of Scripture is not achieved in practice (even if Cranmer's aims are acknowledged in them). However there is nothing to stop churches devising schemes whereby other parts of Scripture are read on a consistent basis Sunday by Sunday. It is not essential that everything dovetails in with the sermon.[2]

Given that Cranmer (and others) recognised how set forms within the liturgy helped orientate a congregation to the worldview of the Bible we should not neglect to use creeds. We may wish to use some variety in them but we would be unwise to use so many different ones that their formational role in Christian discipleship is lost. Similarly set prayers of confession teach us what sin and repentance are all about.

Many churches now use a variety of people to lead their congregational prayers. This is possible because of the higher educational standards that exist nowadays in comparison with centuries past. However once again we must remember that there are dangers in this. If those who lead God's people in prayer do not allow the Bible's priorities to shape their intercessions then unhelpful models of prayer are set before the congregation, and these in turn are then established within the people's hearts and minds. That is why it is worth continuing to use set prayers like the collects. These prayers provide reliable models of how to pray biblically, and modern language versions of the 1662 Prayer Book collects are available.[3]

One of the areas of controversy which provided impetus for liturgical reform during the 20th century was the issue of language. We still have echoes of this today. Evangelicals writing in the 1960s thought carefully about this. Thus one writer acknowledged the need to deal with archaism, verbosity and what he called 'parsonical language'. However he warned that those who complained about the unintelligibility of the Prayer Book may not have diagnosed the real disease. He argued that unintelligibility could be simply a symptom of ignorance of the Bible. If that was the case then the real problem lay in a failure in the church's preaching and teaching ministry. One also cannot avoid the reality that a Christian meeting which sets out the truths of the gospel will put off some, not because they do not

---

[2] See for example Scott Newling, 'Devoted to the public reading of Scripture', *The Briefing (UK edition)* vol 390 (March 2011) pp 15-26.

[3] See for example the *English Prayer Book* available at http://www.churchsociety.org/ publications/englishprayerbook/EPB_Collects.asp

understand what is being said, but because they resist the spiritual challenge which the Christian message brings. We cannot avoid services which teach theology.[4]

Songs were not so prominent in the mind of Cranmer when he was working on the Prayer Book, although they were not entirely absent from his view. Since then their place in church meetings has grown enormously. Their role today should really be the subject of another study but we can note here that they must conform to the biblical principles which Cranmer worked with. They should be based on the great truths of the gospel and be a means of encouraging one another in the way that Colossians 3:16 envisages. The psalms of course remind us that singing is also a response to the character and actions of Almighty God. However it may be better to think of this as a setting forth of God's praise rather than an offering of praise to God, given the sense in which such offering may be misunderstood.

Another feature of modern life is the proliferation of services for special occasions. We have discussed what are called family services above, however we may also have services which take place on a particular Sunday or for a particular occasion. Harvest festivals and Remembrance Sunday are the most obvious examples. However there are also special services for children (e.g. Christingle), carol services, anniversary services, guest services and so on. It is good to have scope for such flexibility so long as Cranmer's objective in bringing people face to face with the living God speaking the truth from His Word is always borne in mind. One might also need to watch that an endless procession of special services does not destroy the systematic hearing of the Word of God which Cranmer so desired.

Cranmer knew that there is an intimate link between what Christians do and say when they meet together on the one hand and what they believe about the gospel and the Christian life on the other. The current extreme variety in practice within the churches of the Church of England, let alone among Christian congregations in

---

[4] Gervase Duffield, 'The Language of Worship', in RT Beckwith (ed.) *Towards a Modern Prayer Book* pp 68-73.

general, is eloquent testimony to the confusion over the Christian message and what it means to be a disciple of Jesus Christ today.

Many bemoan the lack of uniformity which exists today and yet know that there can now be no return to the 1662 *Book of Common Prayer*. Nevertheless to address this confusion it is always possible to take up the biblical principles that Cranmer used in designing the services of Morning and Evening Prayer. If those who are responsible for leading Christian meetings in our churches today understood these principles clearly then we would discover how adapted forms of these services could once again be a powerful means of enabling the gospel of Christ and the Word of God to shape the lives of many.

Latimer Publications

Latimer Studies

LS 01	The Evangelical Anglican Identity Problem	Jim Packer
LS 02	The ASB Rite A Communion: A Way Forward	Roger Beckwith
LS 03	The Doctrine of Justification in the Church of England	Robin Leaver
LS 04	Justification Today: The Roman Catholic and Anglican Debate	R. G. England
LS 05/06	Homosexuals in the Christian Fellowship	David Atkinson
LS 07	Nationhood: A Christian Perspective	O. R. Johnston
LS 08	Evangelical Anglican Identity: Problems and Prospects	Tom Wright
LS 09	Confessing the Faith in the Church of England Today	Roger Beckwith
LS 10	A Kind of Noah's Ark? The Anglican Commitment to Comprehensiveness	Jim Packer
LS 11	Sickness and Healing in the Church	Donald Allister
LS 12	Rome and Reformation Today: How Luther Speaks to the New Situation	James Atkinson
LS 13	Music as Preaching: Bach, Passions and Music in Worship	Robin Leaver
LS 14	Jesus Through Other Eyes: Christology in a Multi-faith Context	Christopher Lamb
LS 15	Church and State Under God	James Atkinson
LS 16	Language and Liturgy	Gerald Bray, Steve Wilcockson, Robin Leaver
LS 17	Christianity and Judaism: New Understanding, New Relationship	James Atkinson
LS 18	Sacraments and Ministry in Ecumenical Perspective	Gerald Bray
LS 19	The Functions of a National Church	Max Warren
LS 20/21	The Thirty-Nine Articles: Their Place and Use Today	Jim Packer, Roger Beckwith
LS 22	How We Got Our Prayer Book	T.W. Drury, Roger Beckwith
LS 23/24	Creation or Evolution: a False Antithesis?	Mike Poole, Gordon Wenham
LS 25	Christianity and the Craft	Gerard Moate
LS 26	ARCIC II and Justification	Alister McGrath
LS 27	The Challenge of the Housechurches	Tony Higton, Gilbert Kirby
LS 28	Communion for Children? The Current Debate	A. A. Langdon
LS 29/30	Theological Politics	Nigel Biggar
LS 31	Eucharistic Consecration in the First Four Centuries and its Implications for Liturgical Reform	Nigel Scotland
LS 32	A Christian Theological Language	Gerald Bray
LS 33	Mission in Unity: The Bible and Missionary Structures	Duncan McMann
LS 34	Stewards of Creation: Environmentalism in the Light of Biblical Teaching	Lawrence Osborn
LS 35/36	Mission and Evangelism in Recent Thinking: 1974–1986	Robert Bashford
LS 37	Future Patterns of Episcopacy: Reflections in Retirement	Stuart Blanch
LS 38	Christian Character: Jeremy Taylor and Christian Ethics Today	David Scott
LS 39	Islam: Towards a Christian Assessment	Hugh Goddard

LATIMER PUBLICATIONS

LS 40	Liberal Catholicism: Charles Gore and the Question of Authority	G. F. Grimes
LS 41/42	The Christian Message in a Multi-faith Society	Colin Chapman
LS 43	The Way of Holiness 1: Principles	D. A. Ousley
LS 44/45	The Lambeth Articles	V. C. Miller
LS 46	The Way of Holiness 2: Issues	D. A. Ousley
LS 47	Building Multi–Racial Churches	John Root
LS 48	Episcopal Oversight: A Case for Reform	David Holloway
LS 49	Euthanasia: A Christian Evaluation	Henk Jochemsen
LS 50/51	The Rough Places Plain: AEA 1995	
LS 52	A Critique of Spirituality	John Pearce
LS 53/54	The Toronto Blessing	Martyn Percy
LS 55	The Theology of Rowan Williams	Garry Williams
LS 56/57	Reforming Forwards? The Process of Reception and the Consecration of Woman as Bishops	Peter Toon
LS 58	The Oath of Canonical Obedience	Gerald Bray
LS 59	The Parish System: The Same Yesterday, Today And For Ever?	Mark Burkill
LS 60	'I Absolve You': Private Confession and the Church of England	Andrew Atherstone
LS 61	The Water and the Wine: A Contribution to the Debate on Children and Holy Communion	Roger Beckwith, Andrew Daunton-Fear
LS 62	Must God Punish Sin?	Ben Cooper
LS 63	Too Big For Words? The Transcendence of God and Finite Human Speech	Mark D. Thompson
LS 64	A Step Too Far: An Evangelical Critique of Christian Mysticism	Marian Raikes
LS 65	The New Testament and Slavery: Approaches and Implications	Mark Meynell
LS 66	The Tragedy of 1662: The Ejection and Persecution of the Puritans	Lee Gatiss
LS 67	Heresy, Schism & Apostasy	Gerald Bray
LS 68	Paul in 3D: Preaching Paul as Pastor, Story–teller and Sage	Ben Cooper
LS69	Christianity and the Tolerance of Liberalism: J.Gresham Machen and the Presbyterian Controversy of 1922-1937	Lee Gatiss
LS70	An Anglican Evangelical Identity Crisis: The Churchman–Anvil Affair of 1981-4	Andrew Atherstone
LS71	Empty and Evil: The worship of other faiths in 1 Corinthians 8-10 and today	Rohintan Mody
LS72	To Plough or to Preach: Mission Strategies in New Zealand during the 1820s	Malcolm Falloon
LS73	Plastic People: How Queer Theory is changing us	Peter Sanlon
LS74	Deification and Union with Christ: Salvation in Orthodox and Reformed thought	Slavko Eždenci
LS75	As It Is Written: Interpreting the Bible with Boldness	Benjamin Sargent
LS76	Light From Dark Ages? An Evangelical Critique of Celtic Spirituality	Marian Raikes
LS77	The Ethics of Usury	Ben Cooper
LS78	For Us and For Our Salvation: 'Limited Atonement' in the Bible, Doctrine, History and Ministry	Lee Gatiss

Latimer Publications

Latimer Briefings

LB01	The Church of England: What it is, and what it stands for	R. T. Beckwith
LB02	Praying with Understanding: Explanations of Words and Passages in the Book of Common Prayer	R. T. Beckwith
LB03	The Failure of the Church of England? The Church, the Nation and the Anglican Communion	A. Pollard
LB04	Towards a Heritage Renewed	H.R.M. Craig
LB05	Christ's Gospel to the Nations: The Heart & Mind of Evangelicalism Past, Present & Future	Peter Jensen
LB06	Passion for the Gospel: Hugh Latimer (1485–1555) Then and Now. A commemorative lecture to mark the 450th anniversary of his martyrdom in Oxford	A. McGrath
LB07	Truth and Unity in Christian Fellowship	Michael Nazir-Ali
LB08	Unworthy Ministers: Donatism and Discipline Today	Mark Burkill
LB09	Witnessing to Western Muslims: A Worldview Approach to Sharing Faith	Richard Shumack
LB10	Scarf or Stole at Ordination? A Plea for the Evangelical Conscience	Andrew Atherstone

Latimer Books

GGC	God, Gays and the Church: Human Sexuality and Experience in Christian Thinking	eds. Lisa Nolland, Chris Sugden, Sarah Finch
WTL	The Way, the Truth and the Life: Theological Resources for a Pilgrimage to a Global Anglican Future	eds. Vinay Samuel, Chris Sugden, Sarah Finch
AEID	Anglican Evangelical Identity – Yesterday and Today	J.I.Packer and N.T.Wright
IB	The Anglican Evangelical Doctrine of Infant Baptism	John Stott and J.Alec Motyer
BF	Being Faithful: The Shape of Historic Anglicanism Today	Theological Resource Group of GAFCON
TPG	The True Profession of the Gospel: Augustus Toplady and Reclaiming our Reformed Foundations	Lee Gatiss
SG	Shadow Gospel: Rowan Williams and the Anglican Communion Crisis	Charles Raven
TTB	Translating the Bible: From Willliam Tyndale to King James	Gerald Bray
PWS	Pilgrims, Warriors, and Servants: Puritan Wisdom for Today's Church	ed. Lee Gatiss
PPA	Preachers, Pastors, and Ambassadors: Puritan Wisdom for Today's Church	ed. Lee Gatiss
CWP	The Church, Women Bishops and Provision: The Integrity of Orthodox Objections to the Proposed Legislation Allowing Women Bishops	

Anglican Foundations Series

FWC	The Faith we confess: An exposition of the 39 Articles	Gerald Bray
AF02	The Very Pure Word of God: The Book of Common Prayer as a Model of Biblical Liturgy	Peter Adam
AF03	Dearly Beloved: Building God's People through Morning and Evening Prayer	Mark Burkill
AF04	Day By Day: The Rhythm of the Bible in the Book of Common Prayer	Benjamin Sargent